DYNAMIC DEFENCE

DYNAMIC DEFENCE

BY

LIDDELL HART, Basil Henry

FABER AND FABER LIMITED
24 Russell Square
London

*First published in November Mcmxl
by Faber and Faber Limited
24 Russell Square London W.C.1
Second Impression December Mcmxl
Printed in Great Britain by
Latimer Trend & Co Ltd Plymouth*

Contents

I

A Year of War

As the first year of war draws to an end, this country stands in a situation worse than most of its people or their leaders pictured twelve months ago—but its situation is better than the rest of the world believed possible a few months ago. Comparing the actual position to-day with that which confronted the British people immediately after the collapse of France, and without in any way minimizing the strain that they are undergoing, we can best realize the improvement by setting it against the background of what 'might have been'—on any hard-headed estimate of the strategic and material factors.

Never, possibly, has greater point been given to the general observation that in war the moral factors can outweigh the physical.

If it is too early to reach a conclusion as to the effect of such new applications of the strategy of indirect approach as Hitler may still try, there is now a well-tested foundation for confidence in our capacity to resist the more direct forms of attack. Events have gone far enough to show that no lightning stroke in our direction has much promise of producing lightning results. This may seem a negative kind of gain, but it is really a very big advance. For an aggressive policy needs to show not only results, but quick results. If anything like the costly check of the last few months had been offered to Germany earlier, the balance sheet of the war and the present state of Europe would have been very different.

What a price has had to be paid for the strategic ignorance of statesmen who could not see, and so could not steer, any course between the two extremes of either appeasing aggressors or crushing them! In their fear of committing their nations to a 'fight to the death' they adopted the futile policy of appeasement —which proved, as so often in past experience, merely an appetiser for those with a taste for aggression. The possibility of curbing aggression was not even recognized, despite the many proofs of its practicability which our own history offers. For the British Commonwealth has been built, not on sweeping victories expensively bought, but on a firm policy carried out with shrewd economy of force and directed to show the bankruptcy of any foreign ventures to secure a monopoly of power.

Unfortunately, our chances of curbing the present aggressors without war, or at least without heavy sacrifice, were forfeited by the unwisdom of a foreign

policy which precipitately swung from one extreme
to the other. There has been no more foolish piece of
statesmanship in our annals than that by which, after
years of retreat, a British guarantee was given to
isolated Poland without first securing Russia's support. It carried the combined disadvantages of provocation and temptation. In the tense circumstances of
the time, it was inevitably a provocation, however
little intended as such. At the same time it presented
the Germans with such an opportunity of easy success
over Poland, and of scoring off her supporters, that
even a strategist less militant than Hitler might have
found it hard to forgo the temptation. The immense
length of Poland's frontiers, the poor equipment of
her out-of-date forces, and her geographical remote-
ness provided Hitler with an ideal site for trying out
his air and mechanized forces with little risk of interference. While he thus obtained in the east most
favourable conditions for his own offensive he was
able in the west to transfer to himself all the advantages of the defensive—since the Allies could only
obtain room for manœuvre, and find a way round
the Siegfried Line, by occupying the small neutral
countries on the flank of this line. Such a course, he
could reckon, would be forbidden them by their
policy as the opponents of aggression.

Once he had pocketed Poland, he was 'sitting
pretty'. If the Allies chose to continue the war, he
could count on either blocking or forestalling any

possible offensive move on their part. Reluctant to face that unavoidable fact, their leaders treated the problem in old-fashioned terms, instead of seeking to devise a radically new technique. And when they ventured a limited initiative, involving a partial infringement of Norway's neutrality, Hitler was able to step in with a far more effective riposte. While they had talked for months of 'opening up' the war, he retorted in such a way that, within a few weeks, he had both closed Northern Europe to them and opened new lines of action for his own use. Then, unfettered by their inherent restraints, he opened up the west himself by striking at the Low Countries—thus giving the Western Front such an extension as to allow room for manœuvre, by his mechanized forces, beyond the now exposed flank of the Maginot Line.

It is of current and future importance that we should realize how far Hitler's striking successes were due, not to the offensive power of his instruments, but to the simple fact that, as an aggressor, he could gain the full advantage of certain conditions necessary to the success of an offensive. His opponents, even if they had possessed equal weapons, would have been denied that strategic advantage. This reflection puts the Germans' achievements in truer perspective. And it should check any tendency to overestimate the all-round power of the offensive.

If one penetrates still further beneath the surface of the war, in its first year, one reaches an ever-deepening impression of the limitations, rather than the potency, of modern offensive weapons—as a means of crushing the resistance of a well-armed adversary. Their power lies in moral effect. It has proved remarkably small in material effect compared with common anticipation.

Twelve months' experience of the war at sea, recently under far more unfavourable circumstances than we ever had to face in 1914–18, has seen the enemy's offensive against our shipping curbed to an extent which is much beyond what might reasonably have been calculated—taking account of the fact that the U-boat campaign has been reinforced by the new menace of bombing and E-boat attack.

On land the attack in its traditional form, and with the customary arms, has become more hopeless than even its most modern-minded critics ventured to suggest. The infantry-cum-artillery mass attacks of the last war, which the armies continued to practise until this war came, now look like museum-pieces. Only the new-style combination of dive-bombers with fast-moving tanks has succeeded in penetrating modern defence—and then only when and where the opponents were short of up-to-date counter-weapons and relied on an out-of-date technique. The direct attack that was normal in past wars has had to be replaced by a strategy of indirect approach and by tactics of evasion.

The war in the air, if it has become the most serious

factor, has hitherto caused much slighter material damage than the most optimistic forecast could have suggested—taking due account of the number of bombers employed, and the great numerical superiority which the German air force has enjoyed. In contrast to the overwhelming devastation that was so widely predicted, the chief danger has now been reduced, except in face of a completely outclassed defence, to the possible effects of prolonged nerve-strain and loss of sleep. And that danger could be countered —as it should have been forestalled—by the provision of deep shelters in vulnerable areas. Likewise, the production of some of the more vital war supplies could be made free from interruption if the work was put underground, by excavating hillsides or adapting old mine galleries. A policy of deep cover, as one long ago urged, would do much to assure a secure base for bold diplomacy or offensive action.

As for invasion, it has become increasingly clear that this could hardly be ventured unless our own air stations were driven back so far that our fighters could not operate over the coast.

In sum, it is by 'counting our blessings' up to date in so many vital aspects that we can find the clearest warrant for confidence in the future. That may not be compensation for what has been needlessly suffered, nor consolation to the many individuals affected, but on balance it registers a definite gain for the prospects of the national cause.

II

Some Lessons of the War

The disasters which enveloped the Allied cause in April, May, and June arose from a number of causes, political and diplomatic as well as military. But one cause stands out—like an Everest of folly. This was the essential misunderstanding of modern warfare shown by the Allied leaders, political and military. Their minds were still resting in the sunset glow of 1918.

During the time that has passed since the collapse of France, there has been little sign that understanding has caught up with events. Statesmen, soldiers, and publicists vie with one another in talking martial platitudes—grasping at the obvious and missing the reality. Once aroused, the British are the toughest of fighters, but perilously slow in learning to fight with their heads—perhaps because their heart-beats are so strong.

If we are to retrieve the situation, we must appreciate the real lessons of recent operations. This nation gains vitality from being a democracy; but its leaders, for that same reason, are apt to wait upon public feeling. Hence it is important that all should understand what happened—and why.

One misunderstood factor can be turned to immediate advantage—while it may ultimately prove the decisive factor. Resistance to aggression was unduly weakened, both before the war came and since, by the notion that the Nazi and Fascist ideologies had given the nations which embraced them an irresistible will to victory regardless of sacrifice. In contrast, the experience of the campaign hitherto, both on land and in the air, has shown that even the Germans are more chary of coming to grips with a resolute opponent than they were in the last war.

On the other hand, the present German leaders conduct war with far more cunning. Their strategy, during the past year, like their policy throughout the last seven years, has consistently applied the method of 'indirect approach'. And even in their tactics they have rarely ventured a direct assault. In every sphere of action, their aim has been to find a way of reaching their opponent's rear, rather than strike his front.

This brings us to a further example of how easy it is to jump to hasty conclusions, which may carry us away into perilous pitfalls. Superficially, this year's campaign may look like a vindication of orthodox military doctrine as to the superiority of attack over defence. Actually, its evidence leads to a very different deduction. The French army paved the way for its own defeat because it failed to adopt or develop a defensive technique suited to modern conditions. It precipitated disaster, after the initial German penetration, by trying to apply an offensive technique that was utterly out of date. By contrast, the Germans succeeded because they had understood the strength of modern defence sufficiently well to avoid blunting their weapon in any frontal assault, while converting to their own advantage that same defensive asset in such a way as to make the Allies' counter-attacks recoil against themselves.

Despite their immense superiority in modern means of attack, the Germans were careful to abstain from head-on assaults, and to press their advance only where they could create opportunities for penetrating 'soft spots'. The most remarkable feature of their offensive was the extent to which it was unmarked by attacks in the proper sense of the term. On the rare occasions when they departed from this rule, their efforts failed with disproportionately heavy loss. Their whole strategy was to find the line of least resistance and push along it as fast as they could and as far as they met no serious resistance.

The Allied leaders failed to understand what was happening. They tried to answer a new technique with an old and obsolete one. In unreasoning alarm they called on their troops to cast away the idea of resisting attack behind concrete lines or natural obstacles, and to reply to the German advance by 'furious, unrelenting assault'. Such attempts broke down before the defence which the enemy had rapidly improvised along the sides of his corridor of penetration—and, by their costly failure, weakened the capacity of the Allied armies to withstand subsequent enemy penetrations. Conforming to old-style orthodoxy, three successive attacks were delivered—on May 28th, 30th, and June 4th—direct against the bridgeheads which the Germans had established south of the Somme. In failing, they used up most of the French and British tank units which might otherwise have been available to counter the next German move.

Before the war, I expressed the view that to give the offensive reasonable prospects of success the attacker would need a superiority approaching three to one in modern weapons, such as tanks and aircraft. The Germans had more than that superiority in their attack on Poland. And before venturing any offensive in the west they waited until, by intensified efforts during the winter, they had built up a still larger margin of strength in such modern instruments —fully four to one, according to authoritative statements. Even then, they took care to avoid a direct attack on the Maginot Line.

In successive books during the past ten years I suggested that perhaps the best chance of overcoming the hard problem presented by modern defence lay in exploiting the possibilities of 'the baited offensive' —the combination of offensive strategy with defensive and counter-offensive tactics. By a sudden pounce on strategic points outside the main front, one might lure the opposing army into an ill-considered advance, and then, when it was out of position, catch it with a surprise riposte. The only high command which showed keen interest in the idea of this 'gambit of future warfare' was the German. Intentionally or not, their strategy in May proved a perfect fulfilment of it. By their threat to the Low Countries they led the French to leave their defences on the Belgian frontier and advance northward; then struck in behind them—with a thrust at the uncovered hinge of the French advance. To judge by the small force which the Germans employed in this thrust, it may only have been in the nature of a 'try on'—but it came off.

When it pierced the French front near Sedan—a front which there was no better than a façade—the German Command quickly rushed the bulk of their armoured divisions southward from the Low Countries, and pushed them through the gap. Their astonishing initial success may have surprised them almost as much as it did the Allied Command, but the mobility of these mechanized divisions made rapid switching possible and enabled the opportunity to be promptly exploited. The Allied infantry divisions, though far more numerous, were too cumbrous to make any correspondingly rapid turn-about.

The more fully the facts emerge about this dramatic phase of the campaign, the more incredibly fortunate, for the Germans, appear what M. Reynaud termed 'the incredible mistakes' committed by the French Command. And the more doubt is left whether even the Germans' vast superiority in tanks and aircraft could have prevailed without the help of such astounding blunders.

General Gamelin pushed his whole left wing, including the British, forward into western Belgium. He left his centre, facing the Ardennes, almost unguarded. In taking this course he acted on the conventional idea that as the Ardennes was difficult country for mechanized forces the Germans would not come that way. It would at least have been wise to make sure—by adequate reconnaissance; but, apparently, he neglected this obvious precaution. It would have been better still to have sent forces across the frontier to hold the strong natural obstacles which the Ardennes provided—but this was not done. Indeed, his own front on the Meuse, covering the exits from the Ardennes, had been entrusted to a few second-rate divisions, thinly spread. Whereas twenty French and British divisions had been pushed forward to support a similar number of Belgian divisions on the sixty-mile front between Antwerp and Namur, one of the divisions facing the Ardennes was stretched over twenty miles of front! These low-grade divisions were ill-equipped with anti-tank guns—yet a part even of those they possessed had been moved away to another sector. Worse still, it would appear that when the German thrust came the French troops had not manned the defences, and were caught in the open. To crown this succession of blunders, the bridges across the Meuse were allowed to fall intact into the enemy's hands.

Having been given a smooth passage through the French front, the German armoured divisions were able to make a scythe-like sweep across the rear of the Allied armies in Belgium—towards the Channel coast. The progress of their break-through was helped by the breakdown of their opponents' system of communication and liaison, which had been organized for slow-motion warfare. The various corps headquarters were often unaware of their neighbours' position, and out of touch with their own divisions. Too often, the penetration of a handful of tanks achieved disproportionate results in spreading confusion and dislocation.

While the German armoured divisions swept on to the sea, some five motor-borne infantry divisions, later increased to eight, held the sides of the corridor. Owing to the fast-spreading strategic effect of the armoured thrust, as well as the natural strength of their own defensive position, this small supporting force sufficed to frustrate Weygand's plan of a pincer-like counter-offensive in traditional style. Only by using a counter-force of mobile armoured divisions might the Allies have broken through the corridor while the opportunity remained—but, through want of foresight, they lacked the necessary means. Their infantry divisions, while heavy-weight in movement, were feather-weight in punch. The Allied Command was like a man wielding a bolster against an adversary armed with a rapier.

The result exemplified the Allies' slowness to comprehend not only the modern methods of indirect attack, but, also, the right way of countering them.

Another common misunderstanding that still survives is in regard to the importance of the enemy's 'superior numbers'. Here, in response, we have been inclined to fall into a trap—by calling up vast quantities of men, whom we can neither train nor equip adequately, at the expense of the nation's industrial activity and economic stability. In the invasion of France, the conscript masses counted for little, save as mere occupiers of conquered territory. The Germans' success was based on the way they had realized, and exploited, the decisive importance of machine-power compared with man-power. All effective action on their part has been carried out by a few score thousand men of the air force and tank force—a tiny fraction of their total man-power. It is true that a million or more infantry followed in the wake of these mechanized spearheads—but France had over five million trained men available to meet them, only to collapse for lack of the necessary modern equipment and technique.

While the Allies had been talking about 'total warfare' as if it meant carrying the quantitative effort of the last war to a more extreme pitch, in putting the bulk of the nation's manhood under arms, the Germans had been thinking ahead—along the lines of the 'qualitative warfare' which some unorthodox British military thinkers had foreshadowed more than fifteen years ago. For when M. Reynaud spoke of the 'classic' French mode of warfare having been shattered by the impact of a 'new conception', he omitted to mention that this was far from new. And that it was originally conceived in this country —only to be left, like an unwanted babe, for others to adopt.

The new current of ideas was first generated, soon after the Armistice, by Colonel J. F. C. Fuller, who had been Chief Staff Officer of the Tanks Corps during the last war. As it grew and spread, with others contributing, it aroused much public interest but also strong official objection and indignation. This reaction may now seem strange, since anyone who cares to look back at Colonel Fuller's writings or my own during the 'twenties, can find in one or other most of the practical points which have been brought out in the performance of the German mechanized forces in 1940. To enumerate but a few from my own books—the point that fast tanks should be regarded not as a mere support to infantry, but as new-style cavalry—'the means of reviving the great cavalry strokes of the past against the enemy's rear and communications'. That instead of artillery support, dive-bomber aircraft should be employed with the tanks. That modern tanks, because of their combination of speed with armour, offered an ideal means of carrying out the 'soft-spot' infiltration tactics which had been developed for infantry at the end of the war. That, if they got round or through the enemy's front, armoured mobile forces could succeed, where the forces of 1914–18 had always failed, in getting astride the enemy's rear before his reserves could form a fresh front. That the inroad of such a force into the opponent's back areas would produce such confusion, and such a crop of rumours, that it might 'cut the enemy army's communications without serious interference'. That it was a mistaken idea that such a force would be stopped by lack of supplies, since it could carry out a long-range manœuvre with far less transport than an infantry force.

As far back as 1926 Sir George (now Lord) Milne, when he became Chief of the Imperial General Staff, expressed his broad agreement with such ideas. That autumn a 'battlepiece of the future' was demonstrated near Camberley to members of the Cabinet and the Dominion Premiers. A tank force attacked in combination with low-flying aircraft. In describing the tactics I emphasized that, given the equipment, they

24

were of immediate applicability, 'not a dream of ten years hence'.

The following year, the first complete mechanized force that the world had seen was experimentally formed on Salisbury Plain, and, in a striking address to its officers, Sir George Milne foreshadowed the creation of 'armoured divisions'. But those were days of restricted military expenditure, so that new developments could only be fulfilled by cutting down the money spent on older types of force. He hesitated to take such a step of substitution—unfortunately, few of the senior officers surrounding him had the same vision as himself, and their influence increasingly prevailed.

In the years that followed, the new technique was worked out and its practicability demonstrated in experimental tests. Among those who took a leading part in this development, special tribute is due to the creative achievements of Colonel (now Lieut.-General) Charles Broad, Colonel (now Lieut.-General Sir Frederick) Pile, Colonel (now Major-General) G. M. Lindsay, Major (now Major-General) G. le Q. Martel, and Colonel (now Major-General) P. C. S. Hobart. It was the last-named who, commanding our first permanent armoured formation in 1934, brought the new technique close to perfection.

At that moment, when our rearmament programme was about to be launched following the unmistakable signs that Nazi Germany was rearming, we had both the minds and the means to maintain our original lead in mechanized warfare. Tragically—for us and for Europe—the heads of the War Office declared their obstinate conviction that 'we should go slowly with mechanization'. Thus the Germans were given the chance to leap ahead. Meantime the mechanized experts of the British Army were hobbled, or shelved, apparently as a precaution against their inconvenient persistence.

This treatment was the more unfortunate for our country's prospects, since the knowledge gained in developing the new offensive technique led to the discovery of an effective counter-technique. But it had taken fully ten years to gain official acceptance for the former, and even then in a half-hearted way. So it was perhaps too much to expect that the antidote could have been approved and prepared in time, unless the war had been postponed until 1945!

III

Wasted Brains

It has been said that 'wars are won or lost before they are begun'. While we hope to prove that this generalization is too sweeping, as we have proved it in the past, it is undoubtedly true that we went dangerously far towards losing this war in the crucial years which preceded the outbreak.

If our belated military efforts are to be directed aright, it is of the first importance to understand how we went wrong in the pre-war years. And how the Germans have gained their recent successes. It is not by wielding a battering-ram that they have forced their way into so many national citadels—but by the use of skeleton keys. In the political sphere they have exploited the insidious effect of a small but influential number of sympathizers within the opposing country. In the military sphere, instead of relying on armed masses as in 1914, they have owed their success to the penetrative and demoralizing power of highly mechanized forces, land and air, manned by relatively small numbers—to technical quality rather than human quantity.

It would appear that three armoured divisions, of some twelve hundred tanks, operating in conjunction with perhaps three hundred dive-bombers, made the breach which disrupted the defences of France and thereby unhinged the defence of Belgium.

The general conclusion which I reached before the war, and expressed in *The Defence of Britain*, was: 'To give the offensive an adequate chance, it would seem to need a superiority approaching three to one. Otherwise deadlock is the natural result. That superiority of course is no longer a matter of mere numbers of men, but of "power-units".' I defined these as being constituted by the mobile force of aircraft, tanks, and guns employed in the punch.

The Germans grasped the meaning of such 'power-units' better than we did. While we followed the French example in raising disproportionate numbers of infantry, the Germans were concentrating, above all, on the production of aircraft and tanks.

Their conscript masses helped to mask from us and our allies the significance of the special skeleton-keys which they were forging for their purpose. It is through the use of picked forces, with the essential character of volunteers, that they have opened the way for their recent startling achievements. The men who compose these key-forces amount to only a small fraction of their total man-power. These chosen men, who fulfil the 'Gideon principle', are represented by the tank crews, the aircraft crews, and the parachutists. While the Allies were still measuring military strength in obsolete terms of armed numbers, the Germans had been calculating in up-to-date terms of 'power-units'.

Yet their conception is not such a novelty as it has appeared to most of our statesmen and the public. It is merely an advance to the stage which was reached soon after the last war by some of the younger minds of the British Army. What the German Command has done is to give fulfilment to ideas from which it was not too proud to learn, whereas our own authorities, distrusting them as unproved 'theories', considered it safer to keep in the familiar rut. There is nothing so unsafe, for a nation, as military conservatism.

The promise of the new way in warfare seemed on the verge of fulfillment in 1927, when this country took a practical lead by forming the first experimental Mechanized Force. Although the command of it was given, characteristically, to an infantry officer, a number of the younger tank experts had the opportunity to put their ideas into practice. And the performance of its fast group under Colonel Pile strikingly demonstrated the potentialities of mechanized mobility. The prospect seemed to be bright when the then Chief of the Imperial General Staff, Sir George Milne, crowned the success of the experiment by the declaration that we had now found the means of 'altering methods of warfare', and would create 'armoured divisions'.

Although these new ideas gradually made headway here, and were put into practice to a limited extent, the whole-hearted application of them was left, unfortunately, for Germany to carry out. Those who took a prominent part in developing mechanization did so to their cost—and the country's. When no longer denounced as heretics they were still regarded, distrustfully, as unpractical visionaries, who exaggerated the importance of armoured mobility in future warfare, and, if given their way, might push the tank forward without proper respect for the established position of horse and foot. Between 1930 and 1937 five of them successfully reached the rank of Major-General, for even conservative authority had to recognize their personal ability—but each in turn, on promotion, was removed to a sphere away from influence on mechanization, if he was not left unemployed. We are now paying the price of this neglect or discard of the men who were best qualified to maintain our original lead.

Unfortunately a conservative reaction soon set in. Highly placed officers declared that horsed cavalry were as important as ever, and that tanks were not likely to be a serious factor in future warfare. Their resistance to progress gained strength from the limitations on military expenditure—which were so applied as to check the development of new-style units, and the provision of mechanized equipment, in order to maintain the numbers of the older arms.

At the end of 1928 the new Force was broken up, and not until 1931 was an armoured formation re-formed for trial. This tank brigade, in its exercises under Colonel Broad, did most valuable work in lay-ing the foundations of modern tactics. But it was again dispersed.

In February 1933 Sir George Milne finished his term of office, which had been prolonged to seven years—years of prospective disarmament. He was succeeded by Sir Archibald Montgomery-Massing-berd, who came into office at a more propitious moment for overhauling the army and putting it on a modern basis. The fact that the Nazis had gained control of Germany three weeks earlier might have been a spur. Yet in the British Army Estimates for the next financial year the trifling sum of £348,000 was allotted for the provision of tanks and other mechanized equipment. Following upon some strong criticism which I wrote about this failure to tackle the problem of mechanizing the army, and a further article drawing attention to significant signs of the re-equipment of the German Army, the new Chief of the Imperial General Staff, General Sir Archibald Montgomery-Massingberd, remarked in a speech: 'There are certain critics in the Press who say that we should organize the Army again for a war in Europe, but I would venture to say that the

Army is not likely to be used for a big war in Europe for many years to come.' Other members of the Army Council and the General Staff went even further by declaring that there was 'no likelihood of war in our lifetime'.

That winter the army's foremost exponent of mechanized warfare, Major-General Fuller, was placed on the retired list—having never been given any employment since his promotion three years before.

The following year, a tank brigade was at last made a permanent formation of the army, and in its exercises Brigadier Hobart brilliantly developed the technique of far-reaching strategic manœuvre against an enemy's communications. It blazed the trail which the German armoured divisions have followed with such dramatic effect. But the demonstration was regarded as unconvincing by those who then ruled in the British War Office.

The continued distrust of modernity at the top was made plain in a public pronouncement on policy which the Chief of the Imperial General Staff made in November 1934: 'It is certain that if we do not go slowly with mechanization we shall land ourselves in difficulties. . . . I am convinced, therefore, that we should go slowly.' Yet there were still only four tank battalions in the army, mainly equipped with eleven-year-old tanks—as against 136 infantry battalions. The Germans, unfortunately, did not share his distrust of novelty—but, instead, were making haste to apply the new ideas which had been evolved by the mechanized experts in this country.

That year a second tank expert had reached the grade of general officer, Major-General George Lindsay; after being left idle for a year he was sent abroad to command a second-class district in India where there were no mechanized troops.

By the end of 1935 we had not only lost our original lead in tank design, but had fallen so badly behind in the provision of tanks as to be far outnumbered in this arm—which alone offered a promise of effective attacking power in modern land warfare.

Seeing that it was hopeless to expect any adequately rapid modernization of the British Army I suggested that 'in the interval', until up-to-date arms were provided, it would be wiser to concentrate on producing the largest possible air expeditionary force for the aid of our potential allies on the Continent. It was a proposal intended to make the best of existing facts, and of the time already lost in tank production, while giving practical effect to my conviction that air superiority would prove of 'decisive importance'. At the same time I continued to argue that even one or two 'completely mechanized divisions would weigh in the scales', whereas four or five ordinary infantry divisions such as the General Staff contemplated 'would be merely a drop in the bucket' of the Continental armies. For a race to gain air and tank superiority we had an inherent advantage, not only in our industrial resources but in the fact that we had no land frontiers. While Germany and France had to maintain, and equip, many line-holding divisions to cover their frontiers, we could concentrate on developing the two kinds of force which alone embodied counter-offensive power under modern conditions. But it was hard to secure such a sense of proportion against the weight of conventional thinking upon our defence problems.

A further two years passed before the advent of Mr. Hore-Belisha as War Minister brought the prospect of a vigorous and fresh-minded régime. His keen desire for progress gave me the opportunity to put forward a detailed scheme for the reorganization of the army to meet modern conditions. It was based on two axioms—the first, that 'the survival of nations, and armies, throughout the ages has depended on their power of adaptability to changing conditions'; the second, that 'machine-power, not man-power, is the determining condition of success in modern warfare'. It was suggested in this paper that, by the conversion of old-style units, three armoured divisions might be created at home, as well as two more in Egypt and India respectively. I emphasized that 'because of their value for rapid and powerful riposte in emergency, if any breach should be made in the French frontier defences', these armoured divisions would have a value 'probably greater than if the whole Field Force of the present pattern were available'.

Mr. Hore-Belisha was keenly receptive to the possibilities of mechanization, but the idea of any such radical alteration in the ratio of armoured units to infantry was strongly opposed in the higher military quarters. So was another main point in the scheme—the doubling, or more, of our anti-aircraft forces.

Even after the partial changes in the War Office staff made that winter, the programme was but partially conceded—and tardily executed—despite his efforts. On the eve of the war, two years later, there was only one armoured division at home, and another in Egypt, neither being fully equipped.

Thus when the Germans applied in May the British-bred technique which the British War Office had so long resisted, we could not supplement the deficiency of the French in the modern means to counter it. To make it worse, the solitary armoured division which could have been sent to France was still at home; it only arrived at the front after the German breakthrough—and was then crippled in a misguided attempt, under French orders, at direct attack on the German defensive position along the Somme.

Why had so little been done to fulfil the high promise of modernization which had at last opened up in 1937? Fundamentally, the answer lies in the way that the mechanized warfare experts were excluded from influencing the development of Britain's military forces.

After Mr. Hore-Belisha became War Minister, officers who might come in contact with him were sternly warned that they must not suggest that any basic reorganization of the army, or any increase in mechanized forces, was possible.

That autumn the formation of our first armoured division was at last secured—the Germans had just created their fourth. The merest common sense argued that the command of it should be given to a mechanized warfare expert. Three tank officers of the required seniority were available, all of them outstanding pioneers—Broad, Pile, and Hobart. Yet the appointment of a cavalryman, of late employed in training riding instructors, was powerfully urged.

In the end a compromise arrangement was made whereby an artilleryman, Major-General Alan Brooke, was given command of the Armoured Division, while he was to be succeeded as Director of Military Training by Hobart—so that knowledge of mechanized tactics might at least be infused into the general training of the army for future war.

It had seemed to me that General Brooke, who had done much to improve gunnery methods, was the natural choice to carry out the reorganization and expansion of our anti-aircraft defences, which was urgently needed. Instead, he was sent to develop a mechanized force of whose technique he had no previous working experience—while General Pile, the mechanized expert, was sent to command an anti-aircraft division. As for the third of them, General Broad, he was put in a purely administrative post mainly concerned with barracks and the Aldershot Tattoo!

That autumn there was serious concern about the tardy progress of our tank production. It led to a change in the office of Master-General of the Ordnance—but not to the best one. An obvious choice, seniority apart, was Colonel Martel, who had recently been brought into the department as third man down the ladder. He combined a broad strategic mind with great inventive gifts, having built the first light tank in his private garage. But he was only forty-eight, and a colonel—while the post was customarily held by a lieutenant-general. And when his turn for promotion to major-general came he left the sphere of tank production to command a Territorial division.

When changes were made in the Army Council at the end of 1937, it was hoped that there would be a change in this knowledge-wasting habit. The hope was not fulfilled. While there was progress in various directions, any radical development either of mechanized force or anti-aircraft defence was still regarded with disfavour. Moreover, it soon became unpleasantly clear that there was an increasing effort not merely to curb but to remove from the War Office the one higher representative of tank warfare. So long as he remained, the 'danger' remained that there might be an acceleration and expansion of mechanization unwelcome to the orthodox. But for Mr. Hore-Belisha, General Hobart's ejection would have come even sooner than it did. However, the Munich crisis provided a convenient opportunity to send him out to Egypt, there to take over the mechanized division that was hastily, and belatedly, improvised in the emergency. All the importunate advocates of mechanized warfare were now out of the way, and Britain's Army had again been made safe for military conservatism.

Similar disregard for acquired knowledge was shown in the anti-aircraft sphere. Here the need for an adequate organization was accepted only two months before the long-foreseen crisis came. With time clearly so short, the case for appointing men who had already mastered the problem was all the stronger. Instead, fresh officers were brought in over the heads of those who had striven to develop the country's anti-aircraft defence—and made themselves a nuisance to the War Office thereby.

There was ultimate compensation in the fact that the anti-aircraft command-in-chief was given to General Brooke. But this year-late step meant taking him away from the Armoured Division just when he had found his feet there, and without allowing him time either to study or tackle the air-defence problem. Naturally, we were caught unready by the crisis.

Subsequently, big strides were made under his forceful direction—and have continued with gathering pace under his successor General Pile, who has been in supreme charge since just before the war. Yet here again the question must arise whether the country's cause might not have gained even more if the vision and energy of this mechanized expert had been employed, during these last three years, in his natural sphere.

Moreover, when General Brooke left the armoured division the opportunity was taken to give command of it to a cavalryman, to the fresh exclusion of the tank experts. Symptomatic of the same spirit was that when it was decided to fuse the Royal Tank Corps with the newly mechanized cavalry as the Royal Armoured Corps, a cavalryman was placed at the head of it. And when he was moved to a command abroad, another cavalryman was appointed to succeed him. While it was right that any cavalrymen of promise should be given opportunity in the new form to which they had been converted, it was unjust, and unwise in the country's interest, that apprentices to the mechanized technique should be given such a degree of preference over those who had mastered it.

But worst of all was the treatment of the only leading mechanized expert who could still influence mechanized progress. Many keen younger officers serving with the armoured division in Egypt spoke of the inspiring enthusiasm which General Hobart had created—just as he had with the Tank Brigade in earlier years. Some more senior officers who saw its work said it was the best trained division they had ever seen—and their verdict has been confirmed by its recent exploits on the Libyan frontier. But there was also an insidious and more powerful current of complaint from conservative generals that its commander 'thought too much of tanks', and was 'difficult' about conforming to orthodox ideas on warfare. And last winter he was removed from his command, being replaced by a cavalryman—five months before the Germans proved the truth of his heresy. The last news of him was that he had become a Local Defence Volunteer! It seemed rather limited scope for the man who had been one of Britain's greatest potential leaders in modern-style warfare.

We have suffered much through the instinctively conservative reaction against new ideas. Since the Royal Tank Corps was the first mechanized, and thus truly modern, arm, it was natural that men of ideas should gravitate thither. That natural trend has proved, paradoxically, a barrier rather than an aid to their prospects of influencing the army's progress.

It is not too late to make proper use of such dynamic minds. Those who were the first to develop the methods which the enemy has borrowed with such striking success are the most likely to lose no time in devising the best answer to them.

Happily, this chain of short-sighted injustices belongs to the past. And its errors have been made manifest by events. With a new régime in power, headed by a War Minister and a Chief of the Imperial General Staff who have both earned confidence by their essential open-mindedness and fair-mindedness, conditions are favourable for a new start. It has already begun with the advancement given to the two commanders who, by common consent, proved outstanding successes of the campaign in France, Sir Alan Brooke and General Alexander. But there is room for all the talent available, as well as a particular need for any special knowledge of the new means of warfare.

IV

A New War Policy

The first need of these days is a cool head. Fortunately, this quality has been, as Voltaire remarked two centuries ago, 'the greatest gift of nature' which the English people have enjoyed throughout their wars.

The second need, no less important, is clear thinking. Unfortunately, the record of our past wars, and the first eleven months of the present war, show that this capacity is not a gift of nature. It has to be achieved by hard effort—of the mind. The problem that faces us in this war is so much more difficult and complex than ever before, that we cannot count on 'muddling through'. It can only be solved by 'thinking through'.

With the collapse of France, and the spread of German dominion over almost the whole coastline of western Europe, we have been thrown back on the defence of Britain. The first requirement is to make that defence as secure as possible. At the same time, our overseas territories and communications are threatened, especially in the Mediterranean. So we have to find a way of reconciling their need of defence with that of this country itself—to cover the arteries as well as the heart of the British Commonwealth.

Regarded as separate defensive problems, each subtracts from the strength available to meet the other. Viewed as a whole, and through really new glasses, they show an opportunity for reviving the historic 'British way in warfare' in a modern form.

This country has never prevailed in any of its major wars through superior mass. A little island, it has never enjoyed a quantitative advantage in man-power. Ever since Crécy and Agincourt, it has always had to rely on a superiority in quality. Against mass, we have pitted mobility. The defeat of the Armada was a supreme example.

In former days, our advantage in mobility was based on sea-power. This foundation remains good. But to it have been added potential advantages in the mobility of air forces and mechanized land forces—which can reduce mass to a bankrupt immobility.

After the last war, in which we had stupidly followed the Continental worship of mass—to our own undue exhaustion—it was in this country first that a fresh and dynamic current of thought generated, or regenerated, the conception of 'qualitative warfare'. If, unhappily, official inertia left it for the Germans to develop and apply, our latent resources enable us to retain the possibility of giving it a still greater development. We have available to us the mechanical skill, the industrial resources, and the oil—which is the life-blood of modern mobility in all spheres.

Indeed, reflection on the last three months of war may suggest that in one vital element we have demonstrated the new values of 'qualitative warfare' even more significantly than the Germans. They have conquered France and the Low Countries not by their superior masses—which hardly came into play—but by the far-ranging action and demoralizing effect of their air and mechanized land forces: which, while much larger than their opponents' similar forces, formed but a small fraction of the total forces. But we have frustrated the completion of the enemy's purpose through a quality, of men and machines, so high that it could offset his immense quantitative advantages in the qualitative sphere.

It is the Royal Air Force, whose actual operations have been carried out by only a few thousand men, that has barred Hitler's path and baffled his purpose. Without its capacity to beat off an enemy twice or thrice its own strength, there would have been no chance of saving our army from France, and a very precarious chance of resisting invasion. To recognize these vital facts is in no way to disregard the debt we owe to the Royal Navy, without which, because of our dependence on overseas supplies, we could not hope to maintain war. Nor does it imply that we

44

could do without an army. But the paramount importance of the air force rests on the probability that if it were driven out of the sky our defence structure would crumble quicker than from any other cause.

That effect was illustrated by our own experience in Norway. It was brought out even more dramatically by the way that the Belgian Army—after most of its air force had been surprised and destroyed on the ground—was largely demoralized in the first twenty-four hours by the Germans' undisturbed dive-bombing attacks. French resistance collapsed in many places from a similar cause. By contrast, the appearance of our fighters on the scene proved such a tonic to the Allied troops as often to make a decisive difference—so that they rallied instead of retreating.

Broadly, the lesson of all recent campaigns since the war in Spain is that troops on the ground can successfully repulse greatly superior numbers of the enemy so long as their own aircraft can prevent the enemy's from dominating the sky overhead. It was, above all, the weakness of the French air force which nullified the resisting power of their army—which otherwise had ample strength to withstand an attack, even if it lacked the mechanized means to undertake an attack.

That fatal weakness was due, primarily, to the paralysing grip of the army leaders upon the development of the air force, which remained a subordinate part of the army long after other countries had raised their air forces to equality of status with the older fighting services. Even when the French at last established an Air Ministry, it remained a Cinderella—hampered by the army's old-established claims, and by the military obsession that the maintenance of infantry numbers mattered more than anything else.

In this country, too, the air force had a hard struggle to secure recognition of its needs. Only in the last year or so before the war was it allowed a share of the defence expenditure as large as its elder sisters. In earlier years its very existence was repeatedly threatened by inter-service prejudices which were expressed in covert operations to undermine its position. The history of those Whitehall manœuvres bears just as depressing evidence of short-sighted conservatism as does the record of resistance to the development of mechanized forces for the army. And the way these were starved, to nourish the older arms, inevitably suggests what might have happened to the air force if those who wished to break it up for division between the navy and the army had achieved their aim. All experience tends to prove the unwisdom of any such retrograde step—though there is a strong case for taking another step forward: to a supreme combined-service staff for dealing with the problems of war as a whole.

A clear view of the parts in relation to the whole would have led us long since to give priority to the air—including anti-aircraft defence. For it should now be plain that there would have been no war if we had kept the superiority in that sphere. Our neglect to do so, during the crucial years when Germany was hurriedly creating her air force, is the world's tragedy.

We are now faced with the consequences.

In dealing with the immediate situation, our problem is a dual one—to repel any attempted invasion by the enemy's land forces, while defeating his submarine and air counter-blockade.

For the navy's part in its solution, there is obvious need for the greatest possible expansion of flotilla-craft, especially the high-speed motor torpedo boats of the new kind which Scott-Paine first developed with Lawrence of Arabia's assistance and the encouragement of the Air Ministry. If we had only provided these in their hundreds, as was urged years ago, any chance of successful invasion might now be reduced to zero. In conjunction with them there may be scope for a modernized application of the fire-ship method which demoralized and broke up the Spanish Armada.

While it is on the navy that we still primarily depend for frustrating any invasion along the larger part of our coastline, the air force has become the main factor in the south-east, where the Channel is narrow. For if our air strength could be so used up that Germania ruled the sky, it might be hard to check a crossing. On the other hand, if the edge of the German air weapon be blunted in the present

47

'high-level' offensive—as may be hoped—the chances of any invasion would be nullified before it was attempted.

Even if no such definite result should emerge, and if a landing were achieved, the invader would be operating under 'air conditions' more difficult than he ever met against the French, Belgians, or Dutch. A most significant feature of the recent campaign was the superiority that our fighters—which form essentially an offensive-defensive arm—established over the enemy in proportion to their numbers. Many reports show that wherever they appeared they easily drove off the enemy's dive-bombers—his most potent instrument in loosening the resistance that he met in his land advance. Another feature has been the excessive losses, and relatively poor results, that daylight bombing attacks have shown where the targets have been adequately defended. Night raiders have been more difficult to check, but their chances of hitting the target are inherently less, while the means of thwarting them are likely to improve.

This experience provides cause for regret that until recently our policy was to concentrate on producing a ratio of approximately two bombers—the purely offensive arm—to one fighter. Such a policy was the more questionable because fighters are both quicker and cheaper to build, and their pilots more rapidly trained. And because it should have been clear that time was short. If our fighter strength had been merely double what it was this summer, and likewise our anti-aircraft weapons, no German air offensive against this country might even have been attempted, and the chances of invasion reduced to zero. Indeed, if we had possessed that scale of strength—easily attainable if there had been a timely understanding of the problem—we might have spared a sufficient proportion of it to make up the deficiencies of our allies, and thereby have paralysed the German offensive in France. In any case, it should be clear that a heightened concentration of effort in the production of both fighters and anti-aircraft weapons is the most urgent of our immediate needs.

Another lesson of the campaign in Belgium and France which must be applied without loss of time is the need for closer and more flexible liaison arrangements between air and ground forces. Too often, the resistance of the latter collapsed because the former could not be summoned to their aid in time to relieve the hostile air pressure.

With the army, the problem of nipping invasion in the bud calls for the utmost effort to make our forces more mobile, together with the quickest possible expansion of our armoured forces. Methods, too, must be adjusted to the *tempo* of mechanized warfare. The main difficulty—which must be frankly faced—is that it comes hard for most senior officers, who have spent their lives in handling 3 m.p.h. forces, to adapt themselves and their habits of thought to the pace of

30 m.p.h. forces. It only comes naturally to those who have grown up in the mechanized arms. We ought to be making the fullest possible use of these younger men and quicker minds, regardless of seniority. There is also urgent need for the appointment of a single directing head for the armoured forces as a whole— to be responsible for their organization and training on a common doctrine and comprehensive plan, thoroughly thought out. This is the only way to make rapid and adequate progress in developing a new arm —as experience has proved in every case.

While it is axiomatic that the attacker enjoys the advantage of the initiative, it may not carry him far save where he is met by slow-moving forces. The advantage is likely to be short-lived if the defender disposes of adequate mechanized forces. The advance of the attacker's armoured units through the defences, if these are in depth, is likely to be slower than the bringing up of the defender's armoured units along unobtrusive roads, or across country that they know. On arrival these can strike the attacker's armoured force at a moment when it is likely to be somewhat disorganized by its fighting advance. They can move up behind a ridge flanking or crossing the enemy's line of advance, with their hulls below the crest and their guns peeping over it. Bringing their whole broadside to bear, they can profit by the advantages which stationary fire, from a stable platform, enjoys over fire from vehicles in motion. They can follow up their fire effect by charging downhill on the enemy, with the advantage of superior momentum.

We—and the French still more—are now paying the price of failure to develop adequately such a modern defensive technique, and to provide sufficient mechanized units for its fulfilment. Both the cost and the danger have been increased by clinging to an out-of-date doctrine of counter-attack. It has been too long the custom to deliver counter-attacks indiscriminately to regain any position which the enemy has captured. In most cases they fail with heavy loss. Such vain efforts are the surest way to exhaust the resisting power of an army. There is more promise in a counter-stroke which catches the advancing enemy while in movement, or, better still, when he has failed to gain an objective—and is thus depressed as well as disordered. Such counter-strokes should be exploited to the full, and backed up by all available reserves, as a reversed form of 'soft-spot' attack. For this new technique of counter-attack, mobile armoured troops are by far the most suitable means.

In conjunction with it, there may be value in a defensive development which I put forward after the last war, when called in to write two of the post-war official training manuals. It was designed to revive the possibilities of surprise on the defender's part while providing a counter to the German type of infiltration tactics. To this end, it sought to give more elasticity to the new method of defence in depth, and to develop it as a trap—by dispositions which deliberately held the forward defences lightly on certain sectors, so as to lure the attacking forces into suitable channels along which the posts of the reserve units were echelonned backwards 'to form gradually contracting funnels raked by fire'. This method of canalizing the enemy's advance might be described as a modern application of the lanes which Scipio left—for Hannibal's elephants—in his battle-front at Zama. The lanes would now be hedged with anti-tank guns.

This offensive-defensive technique is a fulfilment of our greatest military traditions, a modernized version of the key method which Wellington applied. It would be apt to renew it in meeting the assaults of a neo-Napoleonic foe.

As for our general strategy, the situation to-day strengthens the case for the method which I advocated just before the war, in *The Defence of Britain*: 'An active and mobile defence, in which the effect of direct resistance is extended by ripostes both strategic and tactical as well as by continual harassing action. This offers far more scope for audacity and the higher military qualities than does the process of battering against strongly fortified positions. . . . It is, in sum, a super-guerrilla form of war, of up-to-date design.'

Circumstances have forced us to adopt this form, however unpalatable it may be to bull-at-a-gate doctrinaires. But we have still to give it a thought-out design.

Now that the whole of western Europe lies under German domination, it is folly to imagine that we, with our limited man-power, could reconquer it along orthodox lines. And it would be worse folly to raise armies which, while not large enough for that purpose, were so large as to drain our essential industries and overstrain our economic strength. Our aim must be to find new ways of operating against the enemy people's will to maintain the war.

Command of the air and the sea are necessary means to that end, as well as the foundation of our own security. Hence we ought to concentrate our efforts on raising the air force and the navy to such a level as to ensure this command. In regard to the army, the main need for development lies in the sphere of mechanized force. A powerful mechanized army operating under the wings of a supreme air force offers the best possibility of producing any military decision. If that possibility be baulked by our strategic circumstances or the development of counter-means, the creation of such forces would still be the best step we could take for shattering any invasion. And for attacking the weakest point of the Axis—Italy's African Empire.

A mechanized army requires relatively small man-power in proportion to its strength. Thus it would be both practicable and wise so to modify the conscriptive system as to ensure that the fighting forces should be composed only of those who are psychologically as

well as physically fit to be fighting men—the value of
that principle has been strikingly demonstrated in the
man-for-man superiority shown by our air force,
where it prevails. Its application to the army would
also be a means towards the fullest possible produc-
tivity in agriculture and industry—not least with a
view to the expansion of our export trade with such
countries as remain open to us. In a clear view of the
war as a whole, every man effectively contributing to
our export trade is at least as valuable as a man in a
munition works, and more valuable than any man in
the infantry who is surplus to our real requirements.

Equally urgent is the planned reconstruction of our
economic system. And so far as is compatible with the
fulfilment of these needs, we should do all we can to
restore an atmosphere of normality in civil life. For
the nation which can do this is the one likely to have
the most staying power.

It is in the psychological sphere that this war may
be decided. That reflection has both negative and
positive implications.

The lesson of the lost battle for France is more than
a story of blindness to the new ideas of mechanized
warfare. The failures of generalship might still have
been redeemed but for the paralysing influence of
General Restriction, General Suppression, and General Suspicion. These had disturbed the mind and
taken the heart out of her people and her troops. In
dealing with a people accustomed to freedom, there

is nothing more paralysing to national morale than to load it suddenly with the fetters of a slave-state.

Yet we are disregarding that lesson in the ever-growing process of multiplying regulations and penalties—until activity of every kind is in danger of being strangled by red tape. The natural vigour of our people, when really aroused, is capable of dealing with any external threat. Our worst danger to-day is that officialdom, for want of a due sense of the vital importance of freedom, may unwittingly use its far-reaching new powers of restriction and compulsion to make us static instead of dynamic.

True leadership, however, must do more than safeguard the spirit of our people against these negative influences. It must provide creative ideas from which a positive faith can be generated. To get the best out of men it is not enough to tell them that they must be ready to die in the last ditch. They must be given a new vision of the future. And a new hope.

Thought should be directed, without more delay, towards evolving a constructive and dynamic peace-plan that will stir the imagination of our people, and the peoples of the world. It must appeal to the individual everywhere—in the enemy countries as well as in those that have been subjugated—by offering a prospect of something that no other system can. It must meet the individual's need for security of livelihood by a comprehensively planned economic system that will assure him 'freedom from want', as President

Roosevelt has defined it. But this is not enough—since the totalitarian states hold out similar promises in their own way. We must offer, in addition, a concrete assurance of rights and opportunities which these régimes, by their very nature, cannot promise.

To this end, we must make the most of the fundamental difference that separates our conception of civilized life from theirs—the idea of respecting individual freedom. We need a new and wider Magna Charta. Thus armed, we could launch a world-wide campaign by forces more penetrating and permeating than any armoured vehicles. A campaign, beginning at home, for the advance of true freedom in all its essential elements.

APPENDIX

An Historical Sidelight on the German Offensive of May 1940

Some Suggestions—made between 1919 and 1937—on a new Military technique for the British Army

1. That 'the tank is certain to play an increasingly important part in future war'. And that the infantry itself must be equipped with small armoured vehicles if it was 'not to degenerate into mere moppers-up'. (November 1919, *et seq.*)

2. That 'manœuvre (by mobile forces) is the key to victory'—manœuvre based on the 'fuller application of the caterpillar track' not on 'masses of men'. (June 1920, *et seq.*)

3. That the penetration of modern defences could best be achieved by developing a system of attack based on the natural process of a torrent in percolating and crumbling away an earth dam—the detailed technique was called the 'expanding torrent' system. (November 1920, *et seq.*)

4. That 'active military operations in the future . . .

will be carried out almost exclusively by fleets of tanks and aircraft'—while the achievement of a decisive blow would be dependent on 'one side being definitely superior in the air' either in numbers or quality. (March 1923, *et seq.*)

5. That 'the limitations of the tank are exaggerated by the fact that its tactics have not been thought out and adapted to its qualities and limitations . . . the tank attack is the modern substitute for the cavalry charge. . . .' (October 1924, *et seq.*)

6. That the 'true military use of fast tanks is to be used in as large masses as possible for a decisive blow against the Achilles' heel of the enemy army—the communication and command centres which form its nerve system'. (*Ibid.*)

7. That the strategical and tactical methods of such mobile forces should be based on a modern application of those of the Mongol cavalry armies under Jenghiz Khan. (May 1924, *et seq.*)

N.B. This paper was subsequently prescribed by the General Staff for study by the first experimental Mechanized Force in 1927.

8. That the best results could be obtained from tank attack, if, instead of artillery support, dive-bomber aircraft were employed with the tanks. (July 1926, *et seq.*)

9. That the best chance of penetrating an enemy's front lay in an armoured force's 'combination of

smoke, supporting fire and synchronized air attack'. But that 'avoidance is better than reduction', and armoured mobility should be used as 'a means to make the art of generalship more effective; to ensure a smoother and quicker passage to the enemy's rear' —by sweeping round his flank or through a weak spot created by drawing his attention elsewhere'. (September 1928, *et seq.*)

N.B. This was done by the Germans in May 1940, by the initial threat against the lower Meuse and the Albert Canal, which lured a large part of the Allied forces thither.

10. That modern tanks, because of their combination of speed and armour, offered the ideal means of carrying out the 'soft-spot' infiltration tactics which the Germans had introduced for *infantry* in 1918. (September 1929, *et seq.*)

11. That 'armoured divisions offer a new "strategic weapon" which may nullify both the gaining and the holding of positions, and by manoeuvre against the enemy's supplies, cripple him without a fight'. (September 1929, *et seq.*)

12. That in face of the new anti-tank guns, the prospect of such an attack would increasingly depend on adequate numbers of tanks being provided. 'For 100 tanks would be far more than five times as effective as 20'. 'In driblets they may be merely useful, whereas in a deluge they would be decisive.' (September 1929, *et seq.*)

13. That both the British and French Armies were dangerously slow to develop the tank forces necessary for their security. (September 1933, and many times later.)

14. That the French Army, in particular, was built on a last-war pattern—its tactics so rigid and deliberate that it was liable to be thrown out of gear by the mobile thrusts of an enemy who met it with mechanized forces. (January 1927, *et seq.*)

15. That 'an alert defender' would have 'a good chance of blocking' an armoured thrust if he based his defence on river-lines and had fast tank forces of his own ready in rear to deliver a mobile counter-stroke. (August 1932, *et seq.*)

16. That if a force of fast tanks once succeeded in breaking through, their infiltration would be so rapid that 'the defender has a poor chance . . . to rally and build up a fresh line of resistance to the rear'. (August 1932.)

17. That it was a mistaken idea that such a force would soon be stopped by lack of supplies—since it could manage with far less transport than an infantry force, needed comparatively few petrol-lorries for refuelling, and had a prospect of capturing civil fuelling stations intact. (September 1932.)

18. That 'a skilful opponent will choose a line that threatens alternative objectives. And mechanized mobility will give such an opponent the power to mask his direction much longer than before, and to

make a last-hour swerve'. (September 1930, *et seq.*)

N.B. In May 1940 the Germans operated on a line which threatened Belgium or France, and kept the Allies in doubt which was their objective. Then, in piercing the weakened Sedan sector, their advance threatened Paris or the Channel coast. On turning westward, it threatened Amiens or Lille, etc.

19. That the inroad of a mobile force into the defender's back areas would produce such confusion, and such a crop of rumours, that it might 'cut the enemy army communications without serious interference'. (August 1934, *et seq.*)

20. That such a force could most effectively secure a lateral river-line astride the back of the opponent's front—to form a 'strategic barrage' shutting off his supplies as well as the approach of relieving forces. (September 1929, *et seq.*)

N.B. This was shown by the Germans in May 1940 when they secured the line of the Somme and the Aisne.

21. That a screen of motor-cyclist troops, if introduced, would be an effective revival—for the strategic advance—of the swarm of skirmishers which preceded the Napoleonic columns in the attack. (October 1937, *et seq.*)

22. That 'the "masked attack" will replace the old "massed attack" . . . masked under a cloak of obscurity—fog, darkness, or artificial fog. Our chemical service might profitably concentrate its efforts on the

production of artificial fog . . . covering a whole belt of country, as distinct from the present local smoke screen'. (March 1932, *et seq.*)

23. That 'by the skilful use of *obscurity* in its various forms, the attack may recover some of its lost power. . . . A "masked attack", under cover of darkness or fog, natural or artificial, has potentialities that have scarcely been tapped'—artificial fog would have special 'promise as a cloak for armoured fighting vehicles'. And that, together with the 'armoured attack', it was the only form of the offensive that would have 'any promise of breaking into an enemy's position, and ejecting him'. (November 1935.)

N.B. The German attack that pierced the Allied defences south of the Somme on 5th June 1940 was delivered under cover of darkness. Subsequent attacks were delivered under cover of a new artificial fog.

24. That 'we ought not to overlook the possibility' that, if the French were led to advance, either into Belgium or the Saar, 'the Germans would launch a flank counterstroke through Belgian Luxembourg, with their mechanized divisions.' (May 1936.)

N.B. This was fulfilled in May 1940.

Suggested Counter-Measures

25. That, in view of the lead that Germans had now been allowed to gain in armed strength over France and Britain, we must face the fact that 'there appears no ground for expecting that our forces would

enjoy such favourable odds' as are necessary 'to make an offensive effective'. But we could still nullify her advantage by 'the development of an offensive-defensive strategy and tactics', fitted to 'modern war conditions and the nature of British policy'—if we lost no time in creating new means and a new technique: of elastic defence in depth by infantry, combined with mobile counter-strokes by armoured forces. (September 1937, *et seq.*)

26. It is 'a fundamental fallacy that strength nowadays can be estimated in numbers of men. While quantity may still count, it is only as a factor multiplying technical quality.' (September 1937, *et seq.*)

27. That, under the modern menace of air and mechanized attack, for us to continue the policy of sending a large infantry army to northern France was to risk it being cut off if the front were penetrated elsewhere. (November 1936, *et seq.*)

28. That we could give better support to our allies, with less risk, by providing a proportionately stronger air force together with several armoured divisions for a prompt counterstroke against any enemy penetration. (November 1936, *et seq.*)

29. That, 'the best anti-tank weapon is another tank'—since it combines counter-mobility with protection for its crew. (May 1924, *et seq.*)

30. That, whatever force we sent, the risk from hostile air attacks on the Channel ports should be minimized by creating a fleet of sea-going barges

which could proceed up the rivers and canals there, to load or unload troops and supplies. (March 1937.)

31. That so far as we used infantry divisions they should be given the maximum mobility by mounting all the troops in handy-sized light trucks, with bullet-proof protection—instead of providing (as the General Staff proposed) only enough lorries, of a cumbersome type, to carry one-third of the infantry at a time. (September 1937, *et seq.*)

(The references, in brackets, are to the dates of articles and memoranda, by Captain Liddell Hart, in which the particular ideas were originally put forward. More or less similar ideas can be found in the writings of other British exponents of mechanized warfare mentioned in Chapter II.

For fuller detail the reader can refer to *Paris, or the Future of War* (1925); *The Remaking of Modern Armies* (1927), especially Chapters I, II, IV and XV; *The British Way in Warfare* (1932), especially Chapters VI, IX, XI and XV; *When Britain goes to War* (1935), especially Chapters III, XIII, XIV and XVI; *Europe in Arms* (1937), especially Chapters VII and XXIII; *The Defence of Britain* (1939), especially Chapter XX.